Translated from the English

Kathryn Rantala

Translated from the English

Kathryn Rantala

Copyright © 2026 by Kathryn Rantala

All rights reserved

Cover Art:
Cover design, cover preparation
by harry k stammer

ISBN: 979-8-9924582-8-2
Printed in U.S.A.

Sandy Press
Queensland, Australia
&
California, USA

https://sandy-press.com
sandypress2021@gmail.com

Contents

Exploration & Study	5
In the Cinder Buttes	7
Ghost Fish of the Estuary	9
Tundra	11
The Variorum	13
Systematics: Mammalia, Crania and Dentition	15
Der Mann	17
Catalog of Retained Materials	19
Dedication of the Halibut Fishermen	20
The World of the Pharaohs: Figures Shown	22
In the Hall of Bird Cries	24
Illimitable Blue	25
Letters North	27
As if they were a Basket	41
Acknowledgments	91
About the Author	92

Exploration & Study

He has been given a chair in that
Timeless University.
The Chair of Professor of Silence.
—W.S. Graham, "Implements
in their Places"

In the Cinder Buttes

Rope of holes
architecture of the spine
uncertainly alight

irregular
various

then he delumes
then
tries for stasis
with the finch

traced by gall
the plaintive long call
of the gull

   *

rain nosed to me
by concrete
in relationship
convex

doors open
animals out
it must be near
matins

*

evensong
the webbed
the mournful
stretched
as all
glories

feathered
for anointment
oiled

to rest
is wood

*

yoke and beauty
my terrible meringue
o the exigency
le cine chrysanthemum

my terrible meringue

*

open close the white hinge

Ghost Fish of the Estuary

Pillory
host for shards
shells
tenants
smalls in peat
in tide
in attitudes of prayer

beneath a wing
a nest
no fish east or west

ground still breathing

*

silt
water sun moon
kiln a bright
round
wound

august
neither stops
nor soon

*

if this were now
it would be
transformation

if I were writing

but
I am

I post myself in air

text me

Tundra

Traveling down the road a man careens into a truck and dies. Careening down another road, another. Blood is wax, the candle going home in shuttered dusk. Thoughts are moths. Hands flutter like grass.

A man beside a lake evaporates. The sun is warm and this will leave him, too. Winter hard, lake gone, the man is less and less the air than frost. He leans some leaves against himself, against the cold which rubs his heart. He speaks, a note too deep to sound. His stare precipitates the sky, the verticals, and to some extent the wind that skims the ox, the hare, the bleached feathers of the snowy owl, low as light.

Traveling down the road a man careens into himself. His brother rubs his heart with hands skinned thin. The sun evaporates. He leans some bones against himself. He leans some shrubs, some lichen, sedge and moss. Some fish. Silence leaves and turns his brother into air.

Traveling in a marsh, a lake, a bog, a stream, the months that warm are hard to find and then they turn and it is cold. Chill inhabits cells, as tight as wrens. A man can die and then his brother and the ground may freeze into its depths. Water sinks as low as it can go and then the sky is shut. Rubbed as raw as casings.

Down the road a traveler. His soul is white. Not a man who signals, or who shops or one to stop before a house, a door, a life. He rubs his hands to candles in his heart. He looks for signs—an opening, a leak, a gap along the fence, some side way low as light. His heat leaves him. He leans against a post. Lamps seek out his features. He sinks inside the layers of his skin. Moths collapse against the glass. Absence rubs on absence like a thought.

The Variorum

Revisions by the Poet

1. An arrow through the Earth
2. predicts the lean of horses,
3. their brightening necks,
4. loosed and circling the Palace at Versailles.
5. Who controls them on
6. a slippery glacial till?
7. These anviled hooves
8. reducted worlds
9. of fossiled leaves and crush
10. intending habitation
11. of the kings of time
12. aloft their gilded passions.
13. He whips the whitening eyes.
14. She turns from windows
15. toward him.
16. An old day begins.

---

1. …. the heart
2. describes the grave,
3. strained faces of the students,

4. of Saint Croix, Saint Thomas, Thomas Merton.
5. Whose
6. the gravel, craw, despair?
7. These turf-tearing …
8. rolled ridiculate
9. *fossilized*
10. … attenuated amber…
11. and of course queens
12. and tortured animals
13. all slithery.
14. Normally she likes windows
15. [not a sonnet].
16. How she dreads it.

Systematics: Mammalia, Crania and Dentition

Features

Specific:

- The tooth row of the canyon mouse is short.
- The lower incisors beavers are shaped like chisels and the upper molars of the long-tailed weasel like dumb-bells.
- There occurs the smallest lift in the branches as he walks below them, as if, though they know him well, they pull back from touching him, aware how keenly and how soon they will feel his absence.

Differentiating:

- More elongate, spare, eloquent, shaped like hour-glasses.

Common:

- Trenchant, depressed, conspicuous as if crossing a narrow bridge, as if at a periphery and remarking on the sky.

Advanced:

- Sometimes reaching down, sometimes taking up, he seems to make of himself a comforting construction.

Adaptation And Environment

- Rille is a long, narrow furrow on the surface of the Moon.

- Sylvanite seems to arrange its crystals in the shape of letters while *Roche moutonnee* is a mound shaped by a glacier to resemble a French lawyer's wig.
- The hungers propelling him could not be understood even by himself.

Review

1. Size alone will differentiate the moose.
2. The great branching antlers of the elk are diagnostic.
3. *And this full view* Auden said, *Indeed may enter / And move in memory* . . . .
4. If he stays any longer into the afternoon, soon we will not know in which direction to look for him.

Additional Reading

> *I am distracted by the olive*
> *rolling away from my blackened sea bass*
> *and hunt for it*
> *beneath a veil of lettuce*
> *and when it is eventually captured*
> *the flat-black hollowed-out well-like prize*
> *bends toward an absent core*
> *and accedes among my teeth*
> *a Tuscan succulence*

Der Mann

Before entering into a description of the teeth themselves, it is necessary to give an account of the upper and lower jawbones. Of special interest to us is their articulated movement, how they support the rhythms underlying speech, as illustrated in the following sentence, in which a man is heard to say to his friends in the lobby of the Hotel Lindenkrug: *Ein Verlust ist weniger und der Tod nicht so einfach*; that is, *A loss is less and death is not so easy*. He goes on to say that he will move into a silence, *eine grosse Stille*. Silence will not move, but he will move into it, and farther on, up to the hole inside that one, the big one deep inside us. Arriving at its edge, he will look down into it, that is to say, into us—*ah, that silence!*—and keep a kind of watch and quiet. What then? What to say and how to move, as if his silence were a house all his own and not ours at all. When he has had enough of it, enough of us, then he will pack his remnants, his silence being one, and depart for-ever. But we will not, we cannot leave the house of silence within us, and after he has gone, what is left will still be left, though maybe less, but not by very much. After all.

Unsinnig! Preposterous! A bird would not do this, nor dog or cat. Nothing that is nature, nothing made by nature or of nature does this; that is, choose a silence of a station-ary sort, as if there is a fence at which to stand and look at everything on the other side and think what might be there as only *remnants* (it is us!), and decide to stay apart. Of course, those remnants grow more or less and change while he is watching and not growing. We sway, coddle, chew, traipse, send our silence and our words from where we are to . . . Where? Only to ourselves?

That man, then, let him go! Let him choose to stand at edges, fences, looking down at us, down *into* us. The sight may stun him, as if a river going through abruptly stops. Or not. Then let him pick another view, look at every single thing, look full on, and if he has his fill of it, of us, pack his little, his more, his remnants and go, just as the hands on clocks move on, arriving only but to leave again, becoming more and more and at the same time less and lesser still. Let him go.

Catalog of Retained Materials

First Editions: *Totems I Have Seen*, pamphlet, 1886, *A Practical Treatise on the Diseases of Teeth, 1778, Art of British Columbia, Vol. I* (field notes).

Ephemera: Documents related to the study of angina as well as the inability to keep hold of oneself; the eruption sequence of teeth; a replica of a Haida mortuary pole.

Materia Medica: Various laudanum dosing paraphernalia, dried fragments of edible ferns, the crushing guilt of the traveler, the disabling void of the past.

Studies for an Initial Draft: *The Natural History of the Human Teeth, The Upper Jaw*, John Hunter, 1771.

Notes: The shrill, sharp hoof sounds of a mountain ram the color of rockface; excited accounts of lifelike carvings in the Queen Charlotte Islands.

Newspaper: *Death! John Hunter! Witnesses Claim Attack Precipitated by Escalating Argument.* London. 1793.

A leather case with a drawing of a totem pole and undated note from Prince Rupert Island, British Columbia:

> upward from the root
> splay elaborates the air
> particularly the Fogwoman
> especially the heir

Dedication of the Halibut Fishermen

Let their craft
move in them
geared down
in water
fog blind
sound guided
in cast community
with hake
halibut

their cartography
of flow
the night migrations
tides make of men
the whole fleets
of radio silence

elegy and
allegory

loom
and lumber

before the whisper
and the candle
lift them
baleful

beatific
harden them
the souls
who feel wind
shelter them
a young man's vision
is all pain

keep them
note them
in advisories
of fate
the vessels out
destroyed
distorted
ported home

in their day
down the water
Lord
O communicator
of nets
catch them
in the spaces
they fall
through

The World of the Pharaohs: Figures Shown

One:
- Stone vessels shaped as baskets in the Mortuary Complex portraying hands holding baskets holding hands.

Two Through Five:
- Three stages of emptiness shaped as vials.
- A load of flattened sacks.
- The Sphinx immersing itself in sand.
- A declining accumulation of gifts.

Six Through Eight:
- A sea of faience.
- The head of Hathor facing every direction at once.
- The moment when the priest stops, not in fetters in this example, but of his own accord, his futility complete.

Nine:
- The ceiling and pediments of the tomb are missing so objects fall into or rise up out of it in ways not only difficult to predict but startling to witness.

Additional Reading

The Cataract

The policeman knows it is the scheduled time for walking up and down the street and rounding corners. He knows and waits. Cold from the sidewalk climbs the statuary of his legs.

For both a short time and an eternity he stands in the alcove of the building, face up and outward, feeling for the first rays of morning.

A day begins. Light splashes the portico. His back against the bricks, he acknowledges recurring warmth—just as, at the rock-cut façade of Abu Simbel, above the cornice, does Papio raise stone hands to welcome the sun god Ra, who each day finds a way to defeat the gods of darkness.

Supplemental Notes for the Second Edition

1. *The Great White One, He Who Lives Through His Magic Power*. Two thousand years after creation of the Sphinx, Icarus said, *I think I can* be *my life.*

2. A field of reeds, a pool of wax, *Ikaria*, the island in the sea where the son of Daedalus fell from the sky.

3. The sun-disk is on loan from the *Bayerische Landesbank*. One colossus is in the *Louvre*, one was sent by ship to London. The totem in Pioneer Square is a replica of the Tlingit pole stolen by Seattle businessmen in 1899.

4. Pick the island to draw, remember it, see it sometime, take someone to be the wheel, the labor, to walk on it. Draw the edges, the fold, the solstice, winter and summer. Make it the thing you turn to when turning is the thing to do. Call your years there The Voyage of Discovery.

In The Hall of Bird Cries

When it is for food.
When it warns.
When it is an outline or a space.
When it recognizes.
When it is alone.
When it imitates another; when it is a branch.
When it is for swooping or for drifting down.
When it is behind you and you turn.
When you wait or when it is a sound among the
    others.
When it startles.
When the bird is beautiful and aches,
when it looks,
when it looks away.

Illimitable Blue

Occasionally the public is admitted in small numbers to an otherwise closed exhibit. They enter silently and allow themselves to be grouped in the center of the room, arranging their feet by small movements, squaring their shoulders under coats, rolling the cloth of their umbrellas tight and easing the points carefully to the floor.

The doors are sealed after them, the room darkened. Then, at a signal, the whole ceiling rolls back to reveal a vision of the sky unlike any they have seen before. The room floods with an illimitable blue! The color excites in them a rhapsody, a waterfall of sensation. They can scarcely control their hands. They find themselves inventing words to describe it—an ecstatic struggle to illuminate the majesty, the immense processions of the equinox, an ennobling of their little band to an eloquent family of the grateful.

And just when the ceiling has once more closed off the sky, they hear from outside, from the gridwork of crusted snow, a leaf crack under foot. Their senses, now so finely tuned, take it to be gunshot. The sound seems to be everywhere in the closed space, bouncing dizzyingly, wall to wall. They squint and cringe, lean this way and that as if the sound could physically strike them, damage them in some horrible way, as if by alert shifting as a group they might save themselves.

When it is again quiet, none has the least idea how to say what has happened.

Letters North

*He imagined a house in the sky built from
Blocks of clouds.*

—from *Sea of Ink,* Richard Weihe

Letters North

    1

This is the forest entangled
the murmuring sun a gap
but flat on arroyo
draw
a ridge of thought

coordinates of contentment
bioluminescent
on maps of science and
mechanics
two birds of mind
metaphor and transport
sic gloria flying *mundi*
of the moment

makers
maps
repositioned deserts
prairies
hills
forests too
close with cedar
west to
by god west
to shining sea

a loss
unreconciled
in the ground

trains
peacock more than thrush
sky Zeus-like
down the mountains

sometimes
I hear a chorus

I mean outside the heart

visionary gardens
hybrid
this far north
inside too
and far apart
the birds
the whir of
beating hearts

I adapt
that is my virtue

land of rain
enchantment
expiratory cadence

grace in peril
calm
the trains endless
the first alike
the last

I was deposited here
by glacier
my ledges
my sweet sound
of nothing
and agree
these are
productive
days

if I move
it will be fast

2

In *The Catalog of Applied Animisms*
I flutter at a light

resistant
pulchritudinous
in portraiture a group of
the remaining

weave me to the other
the border
like a flag

not that one

much to carry
stateless
the country disappeared

in *The Big Book of*
Early Extinctions
simply being breaks the heart
runs the air
from sentences
from inventories
of the sublime

intimate
remote

strange storage
or portions of
the mute ecstatic air

summer of despair

the rootless
leave
and stay

call if you get through

3

less tilt
than irritation of the sun
Northern Lights
the plasma
smears
designs
do we even need ourselves

daylight
measured side to side
a mathematical solution
inelegant
wide
tonight the Borealis
tomorrow field notes of heaven

an otter slips into the lake
a surface
shown us by the moon

who *are* the very near

which leads me
back into myself
to gratitude
where I keep it

I have never seen such lights

4

South Volcano Road
blocked for survey

men
math
tripod
a holy family needling
for assumption
positing the mark
of silence
of dark

magnetic horses
and a lark

looking for
the magma toes of sphynxes
flowed from vast
vermilion
holds

we all
sometimes
hope for the ecstatic
but no
the common reach
of mud
these political days

road without end
amen
ends here

raptors measure
my materiality
in basins salt/sweet
in white/dead bays
slurried grief
spent mountain
ruined peak
emptied of the need to speak
soul-sized
precise to pressure
to surprise

fossil goo
spewed from cones

all I visit gone

5

barnacles
the patent/
patient moss
siphon water
eat paint
and under us
the dark rotates
with earth I know

I row and row

parts of day delineated
by loon
bullhead
fish
intermittent harm

by night
the campfires lethal
warm

heart
indifferent to the span
and anyway
largely
missing

no pity in it

I ask

*is where you are
how far we come
for beauty*

6

I revert
to sing-song

unhappiness across the nation
disembarked at Skagit Station

unloading stores of
disappointment
for the geese
erupting white
in buffed
artistic
light
for singing choirs
of Covid

the unwanted
to and from
the same
then snaked along
the winded coast
confusion
in the gauge

nostalgia
one wilderness
to another

and in the film
of what we dream
we are

*Clark will be coming
to rescue me*
Meriwether Lewis says
on his way
from everything
to nothing

a tree
hangs over
his dappled mind
geologies of time
vein through rock

turn pale
into
trail

this cabin
he says
has a good lawn

*I'll go
to sleep
with my guns on*

As if they were a Basket

(a poem elaborated by nature and science)

It's possible to ring up the mirage island.

*Goethe traveled in Africa in '26
disguised as Gide and saw everything.*

—two lines in *The Great Enigma*
by Thomas Tranströmer,
translated by Robin Fulton

. . . who shall say that either in myth or history, fact or fancy, about . . . even so utilitarian a subject as teeth, there does not breathe the atmosphere of romance?

— T. Wingate Todd,
The Romance of Teeth

As if they were a Basket

As I am as were a born thing,
as near the mouse as wing
in such latitudes as thin the bones

and as the snowy owl or bee,
framed by the geometries
of beak, tooth, nail,
the fading call in hallways—
      referential as a peach,
      insistent as eclipse
      eccentric at the core—

and as camel, bird, bison, fish,
antelope, fox and mole
cross longitudes and roads,
safe as thistle,

companied by ghosts
and the slyly misdirected
      (how pavement burns them forward,
      thirsty as a willow root
      and bent,
      longing not the same as moving)
cascading noiseless solitudes
of blithe array;

our skin sea-planked,
consistent with the long light,
drawn home foundering
in a strange comfort.

As they, as any, as I
and as a cow beneath a tree,

all shine erasing from the air
hard struck;

the attenuating sky
the phosphor sea, undulate
the bourne beneath the grove,
green feast danced to death by elms;

as ashes bear the ash
in their constituency
as if they were a basket.

[a. – ff.] Verse; successive lines of the poem

Elaborations

Annotations

(See *Citations* at the end for the source for each paragraph quoted in Elaborations and Annotations)

a.   As I am as were a born thing,

I have been spending my afternoons gathering driftwood and observing birds.

b.   as near the mouse as wing

No one realized more fully than I what a chance we took. If the expedition were a failure I never could face those loyal men and women I had persuaded to back it with their faith and dollars. I remarked as much to Professor Osborn at our last meeting. He put his hand on my shoulder and said, 'Nonsense, Roy. The fossils are there. I know they are. Go and find them.'

... well able to ride bare-backed at a fast gallop without falling off, I invite the reader, mounted too, albeit on nothing but a [sic] imaginary animal, to follow me a league or so from the gate to some spot where the land rises to a couple or three feet above the surrounding level.

[Parallelism] is descriptive rather than explanatory and refers to the fact that distinct groups of common origin frequently evolve in much the same direction after the discontinuity between them has arisen.

c.   in such latitudes as thin the bones

And so the two ... began their years of lonely wandering in the tropical wilderness.

[The] inaccessible has a mysterious power of attraction. One wants to try every possibility and at least make an attempt, even if success is not very likely.

They set out together with two buckets, various jars, boxes and test-tubes, a narrow trowel and several pairs of tweezers.

It is characteristic of a good scientific theory that it makes no more assumptions than are needed to explain the facts under consideration and predict a few more.

d.   and as the snowy owl or bee,

Pheasants they found there nearly as big as a peacock, and having tails of 7 to 10 palms in length; and besides them other pheasants in aspect like our own, and birds of many other kinds, and of beautiful variegated plumage.

The crocodile and the boa have the freedom of the river, and the jaguar, the peccary, the tapir and the apes roam the forest without fear and without danger; they dwell here as in their rightful inheritance....

Where on the plain the ground is covered with gregarious and uniform plants ....

And the colours of the birds, the fish, even the crayfish (sky blue and yellow).

Every group has duration.

e. framed by the geometries/ of beak, tooth, nail,

It soon developed that they were not in the glade nor the thicket.

... the room was full of rustling, as though it was packed with birds.

He set up his microscope, and began to make labels. He moved things from day to day from drawer to drawer as he found himself with a plethora of beetles or a sudden plague of frogs.

The clock hands spun around. The hourglass scattered its sand. The distant roar of mines, mills, and ports beat against the window. Footfalls echoed away. The loving and the lost were all long since asleep. My room became an island in the cosmos; this was where the light burned for my solitary thinking, my questions, and my guessing.

If we reflect first on the different stages of the pleasure which nature affords, we find that the first is independent of our insight into the workings of its powers, indeed almost independent of the actual character of the area in which we find ourselves.

… if force can be conserved in one situation all the more energy is set free for the upkeep of the rest.

f.	the fading call in hallways—

He sat on a low bench, overhung with trailing vines and a wandering passion flower.

After a dinner of delicious kuka (crab) we were sitting listening to the wind howl through the tall coconut palm trees when suddenly the hanging lanterns began to sway to-and-fro and the house started to shake.

At length the evening got very cold, and I became very sleepy and determined to turn in, leaving orders to my boys, who slept nearer the door, to wake me in case the house was in danger of falling.

The volatile elements of organized material may be distilled away, leaving a residue of carbon to record the form of the object.

How vast the forces at work really can only be properly appreciated when, after feeling their effects, we look abroad over the wide expanse of hill and valley, plain and mountain, and thus realize in a slight degree the immense mass of matter heaved and shaken.

Comparisons of this sort are valuable for the establishment of chronological relationships between sites and areas.

g.   referential as a peach,

In August the peach blossomed.

Time-consuming matching of fragments ... and minute study ... has allowed extraction of far more information than seemed possible at first.

h.   insistent as eclipse

Now came flash after stabbing flash amid a roaring of rain, and heavy thunder that rolled on till its last echoes were swallowed up in vast detonations which jarred the walls.

Still later, a mother appeared with a child who had been stung by a jellyfish a day or so ago while swimming.

Because of this, they said, spirits entered his body and his stomach became large, and eventually he died.

This morning, Sunday, the church bells were ringing so loudly they woke me up.

More material would no doubt change the averages for proportions and for angles.... The writer does not believe, however, that larger series would modify the conclusions to any great extent.

i.   eccentric at the core—

On such days in July and on any mild misty morning, standing on the mound within the moat I would listen to the sounds from the wide open plain, and they were sounds of spring—the constant drumming and rhythmic cries of the spur-wing lapwings engaged in their social meetings and "dances," and the song of the pipit soaring high up and pouring out its thick prolonged strains as it slowly floated downwards to the earth.

It was in his mind that above all, he must keep faith with himself, whatever the cost.

… inhabitants declare [the two-toed anteater] never eats in captivity, but licks its tiny paws and pines to death. When the traveler secured his first specimen, he sent for a nest of ants and honey, eggs, and milk, but all in vain, for the creature mournfully licked its paws and appeared to resign itself to the inevitable. A wasp's nest was brought and immediately the drooping spirits revived and the little captive, sitting like a squirrel, hungrily drew the nymphaea from the nest and prepared to enjoy a hearty meal.

Recall that for breakage to occur, critical stress must be achieved.

For what purpose it is done, I am quite unable to form even the most remote conjecture.

Silver spruces bordered the base of a precipitous wall that rose loftily. Caves indented its surface, and there were no detached ledges or weathered sections that might dislodge a stone. The level ground, beyond the spruces, dropped down into a little ravine. There was one dense line of slender aspens from which came the low splashing of water. And the terrace, lying open to the west, afforded unobstructed view of the valley of green treetops.

This is mere speculation. What, however, is not speculation but matter of record is the difficulty of the conditions under which the work was carried on.

j. and as camel, bird, bison, fish,
    antelope, fox and mole

... the wild luxuriance, the frolicking and joyous coatis, agoutis and sloths, the gaudy trogons, motmots, woodpeckers, chiming thrushes, parrots, manakins and butterflies ...

... the variability of the phenomena may be too great and too general to permit of being represented by a single set of elements and associations.

k.	cross longitudes and roads,

I was feeling weak and depressed when I came down from London one November evening to the south coast: the sea, the clear sky, the bright colors of the afterglow kept me too long on the front in an east wind in that low condition….

Although the dark in the tropics comes with many gradual steps and by no means at one stride, The Ancient Mariner to the contrary, notwithstanding, before long the light began to fade and darkness was almost on us.

When the leste [wind] comes from the east, it carries such extreme heat over three hundred miles of ocean that the island populace seek underground refuge.

In not a few instances it will be impossible to establish any ideal abstraction….

1.   safe as thistle,

The land high and hilly and covered with wood to the summits of the highest mountains with several spots of snow on the tops. The wind blowing excessive hard from the north.

While trying to flee he was shot in the shoulder by one of the native policeman, but he managed to get away.

We did not return on board till late in the evening, for we staid [sic] *a long time in the lagoon, examining ... the gigantic shells of the chama, into which, if a man were to put his hand, he would not, as long as the animal lives, be able to withdraw it.*

The general harmony of form, the problems of whether there is an original form in plants, which is now manifest in thousands of mutations, the distribution of these forms over the earth, the various impressions of cheerfulness or melancholy which the world of plants makes on sensitive minds; even the trunks of the trees, which seem to be inorganic, and the living carpet of plants, gently covering as it were the skeleton with flesh, all these seem to me to be objects worth further reflection and still [are] quite untouched.

... during an interval of comparative ease, I fell into recollections of my childhood, and at once I had that far, that forgotten past with me again as I had never previously had it.

The market-place was empty, but many large black and white vulturine crows were soaring and flying over it.

Each man held a short round broom, much like the kind that witches are supposed to carry; with this he slowly swept half-circles in front of him, pushing the leaves and scraps to the circumference. Every little while all five men would hitch forward very gently, so that the growing front line of leaves and rubbish was almost imperceptibly pushed out toward the gutter.

… one lives under the curse of the descendants of Adam, who was condemned to earn his living by the sweat of his brow.

We will return to this question later.

m.   companied by ghosts

... the water was still as a floor. Many little fish were breaking the surface. Large bats, about eighteen inches across the wings, were flying about.

Unreal, ethereal, its color a pale yellow in the dawn, with a delicate mistiness thrown over it, it was like a city not built with hands.

Antonio Stradivari had been dead nearly thirty-nine years and was all but forgotten.

Apart from these groups there is also a collection of Stone Age discoveries. These are not included in the calculations.

Bishop Gunnerus [1767] expresses the opinion that the Lapp has his origin in the Samoyed and he doubts the correctness of the opinion of O.E. Rudbeck, Jr., that there is a connexion with the tribes of Israel.

Tooth growth can be studied as a conventional problem of ontogenetic allometry, but that aspect is irrelevant here.

n.   and the slyly misdirected

At twilight, the nomads paused to set up their yurts ... a collapsible framework of wooden lattice covered with a thick felt (a natural conductor of heat and cool [air]) *and heavy white canvas lashed with ropes.*

Not since 1900 had Peking experienced [such] *a dust storm. Whipped by winds sweeping across the arid plateau of Mongolia and northwestern China after fourteen rainless months, its yellow haze reached as far south as Shanghai and hovered sixty-five miles out to sea.*

The afternoon we found the wreck the tide was low, the sea was high, and the jagged points of steel ribs and beams that showed now and then in the hollow of the waves were exceedingly unattractive.

Orderliness prevails in the dentition.

o. (how pavement burns them forward,

When standing in the middle of one of these desert plains and looking towards the interior, the view is generally bounded by the escarpment of another plain, rather higher, but equally level and desolate; and in every other direction the horizon is indistinct from the trembling mirage which seems to rise from the heated surface.

Ever since nine o'clock in the morning the tiny square in front of Saint Sigismondo had been black with people. The sun shone with brilliance, permeating every fiber of one's body. Though it was still mid-morning, the cobblestones seemed to direct the sun's rays back to one's feet and legs.

After wandering about for some time I made a bargain for a horse which turned out a very bad one (memo: never bargain for a horse without seeing him again).

… such a scheme represents merely a momentary hypothesis subject to change with the acquisition of new facts or better-documented interpretations.

p.　　　　　thirsty as a willow root

The men who were scurrying back and forth carried letter-files and documents under their arms; all or almost all of them wore a lofty, proud expression.

My ideas on the dance were to express the feelings and emotions of humanity.

I was extremely unhappy. My dreams, my ideals, my ambition: all seemed futile. I made very few friends in the company. I used to go about behind the scenes with a book of Marcus Aurelius.

At present the annual rainfall is only 6 inches (Hewes, 1946), with a salt desert shrub and vegetation around the water courses and sloughs.

Due to the diversity of subject matter, as well as the cost of publication, annotation by abstract or appraisal was considered impossible.

63

q.   and bent,

Suddenly from the mouth of the canyon rang out a clear, sharp report of a rifle. Echoes clapped. Then followed a piercingly high yell of anguish, quickly breaking.

More rattling shots disturbed the noonday quiet.

Like a flash the blue barrel of his rifle gleamed level and he shot once—twice.

But, as guarded as his action was, the first horse detected it.

… we see that the entire picture of horse evolution looks much more like a bush than it does a single-stemmed pine tree.

There are no satisfactory human data, so far as I know, to give a concrete example of this point.

r.   longing not the same as moving)

But death, while it hovered over him, did not descend ... gathering himself together, [he] *turned to the horses, attended by his pale comrades.*

She passed through a huge low-ceiling chamber, like the inside of a fort, and into a smaller one where a bright wood-fire blazed in an old open fireplace, and from this into her own room.

Then at last she bolted. For several days no one had any idea where she was until she rang up, asking to be fetched from Mont St. Michel.

When she was opened up her appendix proved to be in a perfectly healthy state.

In the first scene in Rosmersholm, I believe Ibsen describes the sitting-room as "comfortably furnished in old fashioned style."

In some instances the factor responsible for these secondary changes [are] influential enough to cause the stable members to be modified also.

s.   cascading noiseless solitudes
of blithe array;

The sea was calm as a lake, and the glorious sun of the tropics threw a flood of golden light over all. The scene was to me inexpressibly delightful. I was in a new world, and could dream of the wonderful production hid in those rocky forests, and in those azure abysses. I could not help speculating on what my wanderings there for a few days might bring to light.

The monographer cannot say to the collector … I have no need of you.

On the walk back the setting sun shot its level rays against precipice and rampart and glorified them. It changed the brown fern velvet on the nearer ridges into the warmest russet until they glowed like polished carnelians. It made one wish one might grow large enough to pass one's hand over them, as one loves to handle the smooth surfaces of rounded jades.

I may here just mention, that I found, at new St. Fe Bajada, many large black spiders with red-coloured marks on their backs, having gregarious habits.

t.   our skin sea-planked,

I believe, too, that it must make a great difference to a child's life whether it is born by the sea or in the mountains. The sea has always drawn me to it, whereas in the mountains I have a vague feeling of discomfort and a desire to fly.

From these speculations one can draw three conclusions, differing in certainty.

u.	consistent with long light,

The room of the Hotel Europa was immense and high-ceilinged. The windows were sealed and never opened. The air came through ventilators high in the wall.

... inward from the walls on each side were short partitions of palm thatch exactly similar in arrangement to the boxes in a London eating house or those of a theater.

If I had never seen it, all my life would have been different.

The distinctions are not and cannot be maintained but there is a real and sometimes useful tendency to use categories differently.

Perhaps we should demand that the archaeologist find another similar ... before we permit either example to be the subject of study by students of culture.

v.   drawn home foundering

I shall say no more about these places, because I formerly told you in regular order all about this same city.... But as we took one way to go, and another to come back, it was proper that we should bring you a second time to this point.

Away in the distance, the others were marching toward the enemy, a long, tired line of them, widely spaced, in the endlessness of Russia. A little dust enwrapped them, and the road faded into the distance. I watched them go.

Conditions become rather more complicated in that part of the embryonic nerve-tube which occupies the head region and which is, therefore, destined to become the brain.

But there is nothing else to mention, so let us proceed.

w.   in a strange comfort.

In the room where the dead man lay, there was, at that moment, nobody.

... the wounded girl's whispered appeal, almost a prayer, not to take her back to the rustlers crowned the events of the last few days with a confounding climax.

My feathered friends were so much to me that I am constantly tempted to make this sketch of my first years a book about birds and little else.

Here the problem arises as to just how exact the likeness must be before the two can be adjudged [to be] the results
of a shared idea.

Measurement of height of head, especially on the living subject, is notoriously subject to variation in the landmarks used, instruments utilized, degree of personal error involved, and even in the differences of opinion as to the feasibility or desirability of procuring the observation at all.

… variance was therefore obtained by dividing the variance between animals by the number of teeth. As some specimens were imperfect, this was not always exactly twice the number of skulls.

It furnishes no estimate whatsoever of the extent to which the one deviates from the other.

This day is reckoned in the log-book as Tuesday the 17th, instead of Monday the 16th, owing to our, so far, successful chase of the sun.

All this is very surprising, when it is considered that five years ago nothing but the fern flourished here.

x. As they, as any, as I
and as a cow beneath a tree,

The prospect was most melancholy: no sound was heard but the dull murmur of the water; the coast along which we traveled all day was encumbered every step of the way with fallen trees, some of which quivered in the currents which set around projecting points of land.

We procured many large pearl oyster shells and plenty of fish but did not see the skin of any land animal but three or four small black and grey foxes. These Sounds abound with sea otters, and we counted 12 at one time with their heads above water, but they are so hunted by the natives that they disappear at the least noise.

In other words, there are two cosmic agencies that appeal to the farmers—the sky and the earth.

There may be another and deeper meaning, but this is of no concern at this time....

y. all shine erasing from the air
  hard struck;

There is a new sound on the beach, and a great sound. Slowly, and day by day, the surf grows heavier, and down the long miles the beach, at [their] lonely stations, men hear the coming winter in the roar.

The traveler fills his hands with yellow fleur-de-lis, red lilies of the field, and white anemone.

There are two circumstances in the above account which appear remarkable.

Geologic evidence comes to our aid here, for it informs us that, at the period when the limestone breccia was accumulating in the caves, the climate ... was rather like parts of it are today.

 ... in other words, embryology in a sense corroborates paleontology.

The larger areas, coloured red and blue, are all elongated; and between the two colours there is a degree of rude alternation, as if the rising of one had balanced the sinking of the other.

I believe that from the beginning of the world there has never been a true or fine school of art in which colour was despised.

z. the attenuating sky

An invisible moon, two days past the full, had risen behind the rushing floor of cloud, and some of its wan light fell on the tortured earth and the torment of the sea.

This moon has changed without any alteration as yet of the weather, and this morning at daylight we sailed with gentle breezes from north east intending to proceed directly to Deception Bay, where we intend passing the severe winter months.

The main point of this paper is to relate the allometric function to human data. The result, I greatly fear, will be somewhat disappointing.

The scope ... will become more apparent with each successive monograph that appears.

aa.   the phosphor sea, undulate

Out of the southeast the huge blue quiet Pacific swells often towered behind us, passed unceremoniously under us, and threw us high in the air, so that the breadth of our horizon was suddenly doubled, then passed ahead of us, and with the passage turned gray and lost half of their appearance of height and formidable power.

The early hours find him at the deep-set window reading the stars which have dispelled the mist and which now shine with the clearness of prediction.

The sediments that flow down to the seas in streams, like the sand trickling through an hourglass, give us a measure of time.

It is indeed a reality, although it plays upon us like a drama upon a perfect stage.

bb.   the bourne beneath the grove,

We push on as rapidly as possible, finding, as many other travelers have found, that miles passed over easily on starting were much harder for the tired men to travel going back.

Titanic wildness and sylvan peace, flown over by white birds ....

When you looked closely at her you could see her lips moving.

It is easy to fall into the delusion that the few things thus distinctly remembered and visualized are precisely those which were most important in our life, and on that account were saved by memory while all the rest has been permanently blotted out . . . [however,] at some period of a man's life . . . in some rare state of mind, it is all at once revealed to him as by a miracle that nothing is ever blotted out.

cc.	green feast danced to death by elms;

It is dark tonight and over the plains of ocean the autumnal sky rolls up the winter stars.

Reality is manifest on many levels and these levels are usually instrumentally determined.

Beyond the widening branches of the lagoon, and rising out of the bright lake unto which they gather, there are multitudes of towers, dark, and scattered among square-set shapes of clustered palaces, a long and irregular line fretting the southern sky.

I am strongly induced to believe that, as in music, the person who understands every note will, if he also possesses a proper taste, more thoroughly enjoy the whole.

dd.   as ashes bear the ash

It is natural to reach the end of a long and difficult task with feelings of congratulation toward oneself and of apology toward others.

And . . . who shall say that either in myth or history, fact or fancy, about . . . even so utilitarian a subject as teeth, there does not breathe the atmosphere of romance?

Some of this wreckage is centuries old.

ee.   in their constituency

It [was] *a lovely, warm night, so ... I lit a cigarette and walked down to the beach.*

ff.   as if they were a basket.

Citations

(Use together with the following numbered list of texts to determine sources per cited paragraph.)

Verse/Line	*Elaborations*	Annotations
a.	(35)	
b.	(13) (16)	(36)
c.	(43)	(15)
	(7)	(24)
d.	(31) (15) (15) (15)	(36)
e.	(25) (7) (7) (1)	(15) (22)
f.	(7) (33) (43)	(3) (43) (2)
g.	(16)	(11)
h.	(35) (23) (23) (23)	(17)
i.	(16) (39)	(37) (42) (40)
	(25)	(29)
j.	(7)	(2)
k.	(16) (41)	(21) (2)
l.	(33) (23) (40)	(14)
	(16) (18) (18)	(6) (18)
m.	(41) (41) (39)	(6) (6) (42)
n.	(10) (10) (41)	(32)
o.	(40) (39) (29)	(9)
p.	(44) (22) (22)	(8) (11)
q.	(25) (25) (25)	(27) (5)
r.	(25) (25) (30) (30)	(22) (32)
s.	(4)	(4)
	(41)	(40)
t.	(22)	(11)
u.	(22) (43) (22)	(36) (2)
v.	(31) (1)	(19) (31)
w.	(44) (25 (16))	(2) (20) (26) (26)
	(40)	(40)
x.	(43) (33)	(28) (28)

y.	(35) (21) (40)	(40) (19) (12) (38)
z.	(35) (33)	(5) (9)
aa.	(41) (21)	(3) (21)
bb.	(41) (41) (16)	(16)
cc.	(35) (38)	(24) (40)
dd.		(36) (37) (35)
ee.	(23)	
ff.		

Citated Texts

(1) A Stranger to Myself, Willy Peter Reese, 2003, Farrar, Straus and Giroux, New York.

(2) A Study of Archeology, Walter W. Taylor, 1948, *American Anthropologist*, Vol. 50, No. 3, Part 2, Philadelphia.

(3) A Textbook of Geology, Part II—Historical Geology, Schuchert and Dunbar, 1947, John Wiley and Sons, Inc., New York.

(4) Alfred Russel Wallace, A Life, Peter Raby, 2001, Princeton University Press, Princeton.

(5) Allometry and Anthropometry, A.H. Hersh, 1955, *Dynamic Anthropometry, Annals of The New York Academy of Sciences*, New York.

(6) An Odontometrical Study of the Norwegian Lapps, Reidar Selmer-Olsen, 1949, monograph, Oslo.

(7) Angels & Insects, A.S. Byatt, 1992, Random House, New York.

(8) Bibliographia Primatologica, Theodore C. Ruch, 1941, Charles C. Thomas, Springfield.

(9) Cross Sections of New World Prehistory, Wm. Duncan Strong, 1943, Smithsonian Miscellaneous Collections, Vol. 104, No. 2, Washington D.C.

(10) Dragon Hunter, Charles Gallenkamp, 2001, Viking, New York.

(11) Early Skeletons from Tranquility, California, J. Lawrence Angel, 1966, *Smithsonian Contributions to Anthropology*, Volume 2, Number 1, Washington D.C.

(12) Embryological Evidence of the Evolution of Man, Adolph Schultz, 1925, *Journal of the Washington Academy of Sciences*.

(13) Ends of the Earth, Roy Chapman Andrews, 1929, Garden City Publishing Co., Inc, New York.

(14) Extract from a letter to Schiller, Alexander von Humboldt, 1794 (translator's name not provided.)

(15) Extract from the Diaries of Alexander von Humboldt, 1802 (translator's name not provided.)

(16) Far Away and Long Ago, A History of My Early Life, W.H. Hudson, 1918, E.P. Dutton & Company, New York.

(17) Growth of the Human Foot and Its Evolutionary Significance, William L. Strauss, Jr., 1927, Contributions to Embryology, Carnegie Institute, Washington D.C.

(18) In Quest of Gorillas, Gregory and Raven, 1937, The Darwin Press, New Bedford.

(19) Man's Ancestry, W.C. Osman Hill, 1953, monograph, Charles C. Thomas, Springfield.

(20) Measurement of Height of Head in the Living, Marcus Solomon Goldstein, 1938, *American Journal of Physical Anthropology*, Philadelphia.

(21) **Mediterranean Picture Lands**, Emelene Abbey Dunn, 1929, Dubois Press, Rochester.(22) **My Life**, Isadora Duncan, 1927, Boni and Liveright, New York.

(23) **New Britain Diary, 1954: An Anthropologist's Journal**, Daris R. Swindler, 2007, Ravenna Press, Edmonds.

(24) **Possible Worlds**, J.B.S. Haldane, 1927, Chatto & Windus, London.

(25) **Riders of the Purple Sage**, Zane Grey, 1912, Grosset & Dunlap, New York.

(26) **Some Quantitative Dental Characteristics of the Chimpanzee, Gorilla and Orang-Outang**, Ashton and Zukerman, 1950, Cambridge University Press, London.

(27) **Studies in Physical Anthropology**, Edwin H. Colbert, 1949, from A Symposium, Early Man in the Far East, American Association of Physical Anthropologists, Wistar Institute, Philadelphia.

(28) **Sun Worship of the Hopi Indians**, J. Walter Fewkes, 1920, The Smithsonian Report for 1918, Washington D.C.

(29) **T.H. Huxley's Diary of the Voyage of H.M.S. Rattlesnake**, ed. by Julian Huxley, 1935, Chatto and Windus, London.

(30) **The Biography of Sir Mortimer Wheeler, Adventurer in Archaeology**, Jacquetta Hawkes, 1982, St. Martin's Press, New York.

(31) **The Book of Ser** [sic] **Marco Polo**, ed. George B. Parks, 1927, The Macmillan Company, New York.

(32) The Dentition of the American Indian, Albert A. Dahlberg, 1949, Papers on the Physical Anthropology of the American Indian, The Viking Fund, New York.

(33) The Journal and Letters of Captain Charles Bishop on the North-West Coast of America, in the Pacific and in New South Wales 1794-1799, ed. Michael Roe, 1966, The Hakluyt Society, Cambridge.

(24) The Malecite Family Industries: A Case Study, Tom F.S. McFeat, 1962, *Anthropologica,* Vol. IV, No. 2, Ottawa.

(35) The Outermost House, Henry Beston, 1931, Doubleday, Doran and Company, Inc., Garden City.

(36) The Principles of Classification and a Classification of Mammals, George Gaylord Simpson, 1945, *Bulletin of the American Museum of Natural History*, Vol. 85, New York.

(37) The Romance of Teeth, T. Wingate Todd, 1910, *The Bulletin of Western Reserve University*, Cleveland.

(38) The Stones of Venice, John Ruskin, 1905, George Allen, London.

(39) The Violin Hunter, William Alexander Silverman, 1957, The John Day Company, New York.

(40) The Voyage of the Beagle, Charles Darwin, modern reprint 1968, Heron Books, London.

(41) To the South Seas, Gifford Pinchot, 1920, The John C. Winston Company, Philadelphia.

(42) Ungulate Cheek Teeth: Developmental, Functional and Evolutionary Interrelations, Mikael Fortelius, 1985, *Actac Zoologica Fennica*, No. 180, Helsinki.

(43) Wallace and Bates in the Tropics, ed. Barbara Beddall, 1969, Collier-Macmillan Ltd., Toronto.

(44) Weeds, Pio Baroja, 1923, Alfred A. Knopf, New York.

Acknowledgments

My grateful thanks to the editors of the publications where some of these pieces first appeared in one form or another: "Der Mann," *Iowa Review*; "Ghost Fish of the Estuary," *Utriculi*; "Illimitable Blue," *Avatar Review*; "In the Hall of Bird Cries," *Siren*; "Letters North" (1-4), *Big Other*; "Letters North" (5), *Utriculi*; "The Cabin with the Good Lawn" (in Letter 6), *Fiera Lingue*; "The Variorum," *elimae*; "Tundra," *Pear Noir!*. Other fragments appeared in *La Petite Zine*, *Blue Fifth Review* and elsewhere. I want especially to thank Cooper Renner for his input in the 'Fogwoman' poem in "Catalog of Retained Materials."

"As if they were a Basket" was privately printed in a limited edition pamphlet in 2008, now out of print. In 2024, the title poem was published by Sandy Press in my collection *My Archipelago*. The authors of the scientific works cited throughout 'Basket' cannot know, of course, the esteem in which I hold them. All but a few of those books belonged to my late husband, anthropologist Daris Swindler. I owe to him my appreciation for the humanity, and the poetry, underlying the sciences.

The title of this book is a nod to the late Michael Marsh, a substantial presence in the wellspring of Ravenna Press, which I founded in 2001. I thank him, and also offer my abiding appreciation to my publisher, harry k stammer, for his generosity, art and independent sensibilities.

About the Author

Kathryn Rantala lives in Edmonds, Washington, near Puget Sound. Her prior book with Sandy Press, *My Archipelago*, was a finalist for the 2024 Big Other Award for Poetry, and followed *A Little Family*, a collection of short prose, from Spuyten Duyvil Press in 2023. Forthcoming works are a chapbook, *Letters to America*, from Louffa Press, and a long poem, "Down by the Humus Lake," at Ron Slate's *On the Seawall*. *The Jack Gunter Series*, 2023, a three-volume boxed set of poems largely influenced by the Skagit Valley, was illustrated by collaborator and friend, Camano Island painter Jack Gunter. Kathryn is also a visual artist, working in assemblage and collage. You may find her work at kathrynrantala.com.

www.ingramcontent.com/pod-product-compliance
Lightning Source LLC
Chambersburg PA
CBHW060406050426
42449CB00009B/1918